50 Kitchen of the Gods Recipes

By: Kelly Johnson

Table of Contents

- Ambrosia Nectar Pudding
- Olympian Honey Cakes
- Celestial Fig and Walnut Tart
- Divine Pomegranate Sorbet
- Zeus' Thunderbolt Lamb Stew
- Apollo's Sun-Dried Tomato Pasta
- Hera's Rosewater Baklava
- Mount Olympus Stuffed Grape Leaves
- Hermes' Speedy Olive Tapenade
- Aphrodite's Love Apple Salad
- Titan's Roasted Garlic and Herb Chicken
- Elysium Golden Apple Crisp
- Poseidon's Ocean Bounty Paella
- Dionysus' Drunken Grape Cheesecake
- Persephone's Underworld Pomegranate Glaze
- Artemis' Wild Boar and Berry Sauce
- Hades' Smoked Mushroom Risotto
- Ares' Spicy Warrior Chili
- Nectar of the Immortals Smoothie
- Prometheus' Fire-Grilled Lamb Chops
- Hephaestus' Molten Lava Cake
- Athena's Wisdom Olive Oil Bread
- Echo's Whipped Honey Ricotta
- Medusa's Stone-Ground Pesto
- Demeter's Harvest Barley Soup
- Chariot Fire Roasted Peppers
- Golden Fleece Honey-Glazed Ham
- Celestial Star Anise Pears
- Ambrosial Vanilla Bean Rice Pudding
- Titan's Mighty Spiced Lentils
- Hero's Feast Stuffed Mushrooms
- Eternal Flame Baked Brie
- Selene's Moonlit Lavender Lemonade
- Nectarous Apricot Almond Tart
- Circe's Enchanted Herb Butter

- Hercules' Power Lentil Stew
- Orion's Constellation Berry Tart
- Eros' Passionfruit Mousse
- Celestial Honeycomb Parfait
- Underworld Spiced Dark Chocolate
- Pegasus' Fluffy Cloud Pancakes
- Pandora's Surprise Truffle Box
- Mount Olympus Date and Nut Bars
- Gilded Thyme-Infused Roast Duck
- Aeolus' Whirlwind Citrus Salad
- Golden Chariot Roasted Squash
- Ambrosia Caramelized Figs with Yogurt
- Hestia's Hearth Baked Apple Dumplings
- Aurora's Sunrise Mango Sorbet
- Nectar-Soaked Almond Pastries

Ambrosia Nectar Pudding

Ingredients:

- 1 cup heavy cream
- 1 cup whole milk
- ½ cup granulated sugar
- 3 tbsp cornstarch
- ¼ tsp salt
- 1 tsp vanilla extract
- ½ cup crushed pineapple, drained
- ½ cup mandarin orange segments, chopped
- ¼ cup shredded coconut
- ¼ cup maraschino cherries, chopped
- ¼ cup mini marshmallows
- 1 tbsp honey (optional, for extra nectar-like sweetness)
- Whipped cream and toasted coconut for garnish

Instructions:

1. **Prepare the Pudding Base**
   - In a medium saucepan, whisk together milk, heavy cream, sugar, cornstarch, and salt until smooth.
   - Cook over medium heat, stirring constantly, until the mixture thickens (about 5–7 minutes).
2. **Flavor It Up**
   - Remove from heat and stir in vanilla extract and honey (if using).
   - Let the mixture cool slightly before adding the fruit.
3. **Mix in the Goodness**
   - Gently fold in the crushed pineapple, mandarin oranges, shredded coconut, maraschino cherries, and mini marshmallows.
4. **Chill & Serve**
   - Transfer the pudding to serving dishes and refrigerate for at least 2 hours.
   - Garnish with whipped cream and toasted coconut before serving.

Olympian Honey Cakes

Ingredients:

- 2 cups all-purpose flour
- 1 tsp baking powder
- ½ tsp salt
- ½ cup unsalted butter, softened
- ½ cup honey
- ¼ cup brown sugar
- 2 eggs
- ½ cup milk
- 1 tsp vanilla extract
- ½ tsp cinnamon
- Chopped nuts or dried fruits for garnish (optional)

Instructions:

1. Preheat the oven to 350°F (175°C). Grease a muffin tin or line it with cupcake liners.
2. In a bowl, whisk together the flour, baking powder, salt, and cinnamon.
3. In another bowl, beat the butter, honey, and brown sugar until creamy.
4. Add eggs one at a time, mixing well, then stir in the vanilla.
5. Gradually add the dry ingredients, alternating with the milk, mixing until smooth.
6. Pour batter into the muffin tin, filling each cup about ¾ full.
7. Bake for 18–20 minutes or until golden brown and a toothpick comes out clean.
8. Let cool, then drizzle with extra honey and sprinkle with nuts or dried fruits if desired.

Celestial Fig and Walnut Tart

Ingredients:

For the crust:

- 1 ½ cups all-purpose flour
- ½ cup unsalted butter, cold and cubed
- ¼ cup powdered sugar
- 1 egg yolk
- 2 tbsp cold water

For the filling:

- 1 cup dried figs, chopped
- ½ cup walnuts, chopped
- ½ cup honey
- ¼ cup brown sugar
- ½ cup heavy cream
- 1 tsp vanilla extract
- ½ tsp cinnamon

Instructions:

1. Preheat oven to 350°F (175°C). Grease a tart pan.
2. Mix flour, powdered sugar, and butter until crumbly. Add egg yolk and water, mixing until a dough forms.
3. Press the dough into the tart pan and chill for 15 minutes.
4. Bake for 15 minutes, then let cool.
5. In a saucepan, heat honey, brown sugar, and cream over low heat until smooth.
6. Stir in vanilla, cinnamon, figs, and walnuts.
7. Pour filling into the tart crust and bake for 20 minutes until set.
8. Let cool before slicing.

Divine Pomegranate Sorbet

Ingredients:

- 2 cups pomegranate juice
- ½ cup sugar
- 1 tbsp lemon juice
- ½ cup water
- 1 tbsp honey

Instructions:

1. In a saucepan, heat sugar and water over medium heat until dissolved.
2. Remove from heat and stir in pomegranate juice, lemon juice, and honey.
3. Chill the mixture for at least 2 hours.
4. Pour into an ice cream maker and churn according to the manufacturer's instructions.
5. Freeze for at least 4 hours before serving.

Zeus' Thunderbolt Lamb Stew

Ingredients:

- 1 ½ lbs lamb, cubed
- 2 tbsp olive oil
- 1 onion, chopped
- 3 cloves garlic, minced
- 2 carrots, sliced
- 1 cup diced tomatoes
- 2 cups beef or lamb broth
- ½ cup red wine
- 1 tsp oregano
- ½ tsp thyme
- ½ tsp cinnamon
- Salt and pepper to taste
- 1 bay leaf
- 1 cup chickpeas (cooked or canned)

Instructions:

1. Heat olive oil in a pot over medium heat. Brown the lamb on all sides, then remove and set aside.
2. In the same pot, sauté onions, garlic, and carrots until soft.
3. Return the lamb to the pot and add tomatoes, broth, wine, and seasonings.
4. Bring to a boil, then reduce heat and simmer for 1 ½ to 2 hours.
5. Add chickpeas in the last 20 minutes of cooking.
6. Remove bay leaf, adjust seasoning, and serve warm.

Apollo's Sun-Dried Tomato Pasta

Ingredients:

- 12 oz pasta (spaghetti or fettuccine)
- 2 tbsp olive oil
- 3 cloves garlic, minced
- ½ cup sun-dried tomatoes, chopped
- 1 cup cherry tomatoes, halved
- ½ cup heavy cream
- ½ cup grated Parmesan cheese
- ½ tsp red pepper flakes
- 1 tsp dried oregano
- Salt and pepper to taste
- Fresh basil for garnish

Instructions:

1. Cook pasta according to package instructions. Reserve ½ cup of pasta water.
2. Heat olive oil in a pan over medium heat. Add garlic and cook until fragrant.
3. Stir in sun-dried tomatoes and cherry tomatoes, cooking for 3–4 minutes.
4. Pour in heavy cream and add Parmesan, red pepper flakes, oregano, salt, and pepper.
5. Toss in the pasta, adding reserved pasta water if needed to loosen the sauce.
6. Serve hot, garnished with fresh basil.

Hera's Rosewater Baklava

Ingredients:

- 1 package phyllo dough, thawed
- 2 cups walnuts, finely chopped
- 1 cup almonds, finely chopped
- 1 cup butter, melted
- 1 tsp cinnamon
- 1 cup honey
- ½ cup sugar
- ½ cup water
- 1 tbsp rosewater

Instructions:

1. Preheat oven to 350°F (175°C). Grease a baking dish.
2. Mix walnuts, almonds, and cinnamon in a bowl.
3. Layer 8 sheets of phyllo in the dish, brushing each with butter.
4. Spread a layer of nut mixture, then repeat layers of phyllo and nuts until finished.
5. Cut into diamond shapes and bake for 40 minutes.
6. In a saucepan, heat honey, sugar, water, and rosewater until syrupy.
7. Pour syrup over the hot baklava and let it absorb before serving.

Mount Olympus Stuffed Grape Leaves

Ingredients:

- 1 jar grape leaves, rinsed
- 1 cup rice, cooked
- ½ cup ground lamb (optional)
- ½ cup fresh parsley, chopped
- ½ tsp allspice
- 1 tsp lemon juice
- ¼ cup olive oil
- 2 cloves garlic, minced
- Salt and pepper to taste

Instructions:

1. Mix rice, lamb (if using), parsley, allspice, lemon juice, olive oil, garlic, salt, and pepper.
2. Lay out grape leaves and place 1 tbsp of filling in the center.
3. Fold in sides and roll tightly.
4. Arrange in a pot, add water to cover, and simmer for 40 minutes.
5. Serve warm or chilled with yogurt.

Hermes' Speedy Olive Tapenade

Ingredients:

- 1 cup mixed olives, pitted
- 2 tbsp capers
- 2 tbsp olive oil
- 1 clove garlic
- ½ tsp lemon zest
- 1 tsp fresh lemon juice
- ½ tsp dried oregano

Instructions:

1. Blend all ingredients in a food processor until chunky-smooth.
2. Serve with bread, crackers, or as a spread.

Aphrodite's Love Apple Salad

Ingredients:

- 2 cups cherry tomatoes, halved
- 1 cup mozzarella pearls
- ½ cup fresh basil leaves
- 2 tbsp balsamic glaze
- 2 tbsp olive oil
- Salt and pepper to taste

Instructions:

1. Toss tomatoes, mozzarella, and basil in a bowl.
2. Drizzle with olive oil and balsamic glaze.
3. Season with salt and pepper.

Titan's Roasted Garlic and Herb Chicken

Ingredients:

- 1 whole chicken
- 4 cloves garlic, minced
- 2 tbsp olive oil
- 1 tbsp fresh thyme
- 1 tbsp fresh rosemary
- 1 tsp salt
- ½ tsp black pepper
- 1 lemon, sliced

Instructions:

1. Preheat oven to 375°F (190°C).
2. Mix garlic, olive oil, herbs, salt, and pepper.
3. Rub the mixture over the chicken and stuff with lemon slices.
4. Roast for 1 hour 15 minutes, basting occasionally.
5. Let rest before serving.

Elysium Golden Apple Crisp

Ingredients:

- 4 apples, sliced
- ½ cup brown sugar
- ½ cup oats
- ¼ cup flour
- ½ tsp cinnamon
- 4 tbsp butter, melted

Instructions:

1. Preheat oven to 350°F (175°C).
2. Toss apples with 2 tbsp brown sugar and cinnamon.
3. Mix oats, flour, remaining sugar, and butter.
4. Layer apples in a baking dish and top with oat mixture.
5. Bake for 30–35 minutes.

Poseidon's Ocean Bounty Paella

Ingredients:

- 1 ½ cups Arborio rice
- 2 tbsp olive oil
- ½ lb shrimp
- ½ lb mussels
- ½ lb squid rings
- 1 small onion, diced
- 2 cloves garlic, minced
- 1 tomato, chopped
- 4 cups seafood broth
- ½ tsp saffron
- ½ tsp paprika
- Salt and pepper to taste

Instructions:

1. Heat olive oil in a large pan, cook onion and garlic.
2. Stir in rice, tomato, saffron, and paprika.
3. Add broth and simmer for 15 minutes.
4. Add seafood and cook until shrimp turns pink and mussels open.

Dionysus' Drunken Grape Cheesecake

Ingredients:

For the crust:

- 1 ½ cups graham cracker crumbs
- ¼ cup melted butter

For the filling:

- 16 oz cream cheese, softened
- ½ cup sugar
- 2 eggs
- ½ cup red wine
- ½ cup grapes, halved

Instructions:

1. Preheat oven to 325°F (165°C).
2. Mix graham crackers and butter, press into a springform pan.
3. Beat cream cheese, sugar, eggs, and wine until smooth.
4. Pour over crust and top with grapes.
5. Bake for 45 minutes, then chill.

Persephone's Underworld Pomegranate Glaze

Ingredients:

- 1 cup pomegranate juice
- ¼ cup honey
- 1 tbsp balsamic vinegar
- ½ tsp cinnamon
- Pinch of salt

Instructions:

1. Simmer all ingredients in a saucepan over medium heat.
2. Reduce until thickened (about 10 minutes).
3. Drizzle over meats, vegetables, or desserts.

Artemis' Wild Boar and Berry Sauce

Ingredients:

- 2 lbs wild boar loin (or pork loin)
- 2 tbsp olive oil
- 2 cloves garlic, minced
- 1 tsp thyme
- 1 tsp salt
- ½ tsp black pepper

For the sauce:

- 1 cup mixed berries (blackberries, blueberries, raspberries)
- ½ cup red wine
- 2 tbsp honey
- 1 tbsp balsamic vinegar
- 1 tsp fresh rosemary

Instructions:

1. Preheat oven to 375°F (190°C).
2. Rub the boar loin with olive oil, garlic, thyme, salt, and pepper. Sear in a pan for 2 minutes per side.
3. Transfer to oven and roast for 20–25 minutes.
4. In a saucepan, combine berries, wine, honey, vinegar, and rosemary. Simmer until thickened.
5. Slice boar and serve with sauce.

Hades' Smoked Mushroom Risotto

Ingredients:

- 1 ½ cups Arborio rice
- 4 cups mushroom broth
- ½ cup dry white wine
- 1 cup mixed wild mushrooms, chopped
- 1 small onion, diced
- 2 cloves garlic, minced
- ½ cup Parmesan cheese
- 2 tbsp butter
- 1 tsp smoked paprika
- Salt and pepper to taste

Instructions:

1. Sauté onions, garlic, and mushrooms in butter.
2. Stir in rice and toast for 2 minutes.
3. Add wine, letting it absorb. Gradually add broth, stirring frequently.
4. Stir in smoked paprika, Parmesan, salt, and pepper.

Ares' Spicy Warrior Chili

Ingredients:

- 1 lb ground beef or bison
- 1 can kidney beans, drained
- 1 can crushed tomatoes
- 1 small onion, diced
- 2 cloves garlic, minced
- 1 jalapeño, minced
- 1 tsp cumin
- 1 tsp smoked paprika
- ½ tsp cayenne
- Salt and pepper to taste

Instructions:

1. Brown beef in a pot. Add onions, garlic, and jalapeño.
2. Stir in tomatoes, beans, and spices.
3. Simmer for 30 minutes.

Nectar of the Immortals Smoothie

Ingredients:

- 1 cup fresh mango
- ½ cup Greek yogurt
- ½ cup coconut water
- 1 tbsp honey
- ½ tsp turmeric

Instructions:

1. Blend all ingredients until smooth.
2. Serve chilled.

Prometheus' Fire-Grilled Lamb Chops

Ingredients:

- 4 lamb chops
- 2 tbsp olive oil
- 2 cloves garlic, minced
- 1 tsp oregano
- ½ tsp salt
- ½ tsp black pepper

Instructions:

1. Rub lamb with oil, garlic, oregano, salt, and pepper.
2. Grill over high heat for 3–4 minutes per side.

Hephaestus' Molten Lava Cake

Ingredients:

- ½ cup dark chocolate
- ¼ cup butter
- ½ cup sugar
- 2 eggs
- ¼ cup flour
- ½ tsp vanilla

Instructions:

1. Preheat oven to 400°F (200°C). Grease ramekins.
2. Melt chocolate and butter together. Stir in sugar, eggs, flour, and vanilla.
3. Pour into ramekins and bake for 12 minutes.

Athena's Wisdom Olive Oil Bread

Ingredients:

- 3 cups flour
- 1 packet yeast
- 1 cup warm water
- ¼ cup olive oil
- 1 tsp salt
- ½ tsp rosemary

Instructions:

1. Mix all ingredients and knead for 5 minutes.
2. Let rise for 1 hour.
3. Bake at 375°F (190°C) for 30 minutes.

Echo's Whipped Honey Ricotta

Ingredients:

- 1 cup ricotta cheese
- 2 tbsp honey
- ½ tsp cinnamon

Instructions:

1. Whip all ingredients together.
2. Serve with fruit or bread.

Medusa's Stone-Ground Pesto

Ingredients:

- 2 cups fresh basil
- ½ cup olive oil
- ¼ cup pine nuts
- 2 cloves garlic
- ½ cup Parmesan cheese

Instructions:

1. Blend all ingredients into a thick paste.
2. Serve over pasta or bread.

Demeter's Harvest Barley Soup

Ingredients:

- ½ cup pearl barley
- 1 small onion, diced
- 2 carrots, chopped
- 2 cloves garlic, minced
- 4 cups vegetable broth
- 1 tsp thyme
- Salt and pepper to taste

Instructions:

1. Sauté onion, carrots, and garlic.
2. Add barley, broth, and thyme. Simmer for 40 minutes.

Chariot Fire Roasted Peppers

Ingredients:

- 4 large bell peppers (red, yellow, or orange)
- 2 tbsp olive oil
- 1 tsp smoked paprika
- ½ tsp sea salt
- ½ tsp black pepper
- 1 tbsp balsamic vinegar

Instructions:

1. Preheat oven to 450°F (230°C) or heat a grill.
2. Brush peppers with olive oil and season with paprika, salt, and pepper.
3. Roast or grill until blackened and blistered, turning occasionally (about 15 minutes).
4. Let cool slightly, then peel off charred skin and drizzle with balsamic vinegar.

Golden Fleece Honey-Glazed Ham

Ingredients:

- 1 bone-in ham (6–8 lbs)
- ½ cup honey
- ¼ cup Dijon mustard
- ¼ cup brown sugar
- 1 tsp cinnamon
- ½ tsp cloves

Instructions:

1. Preheat oven to 325°F (165°C).
2. Score the ham and place in a roasting pan.
3. Mix honey, mustard, brown sugar, cinnamon, and cloves. Brush over ham.
4. Bake for 1.5–2 hours, basting every 30 minutes.

Celestial Star Anise Pears

Ingredients:

- 4 ripe pears, peeled and halved
- 2 cups red wine
- ½ cup sugar
- 2 star anise
- 1 cinnamon stick
- 1 tsp vanilla extract

Instructions:

1. In a saucepan, combine wine, sugar, star anise, cinnamon, and vanilla.
2. Bring to a simmer, then add pears.
3. Poach for 20 minutes, turning pears occasionally.
4. Serve warm with syrup drizzled over.

Ambrosial Vanilla Bean Rice Pudding

Ingredients:

- ¾ cup Arborio rice
- 3 cups milk
- ½ cup heavy cream
- ½ cup sugar
- 1 vanilla bean (or 1 tsp vanilla extract)
- ½ tsp cinnamon

Instructions:

1. In a saucepan, combine rice, milk, cream, and sugar.
2. Split the vanilla bean and scrape out the seeds. Add to the pot.
3. Simmer over low heat, stirring, until rice is soft and thick (about 25 minutes).
4. Sprinkle with cinnamon before serving.

Titan's Mighty Spiced Lentils

Ingredients:

- 1 cup lentils
- 4 cups vegetable broth
- 1 small onion, diced
- 2 cloves garlic, minced
- 1 tsp cumin
- 1 tsp turmeric
- ½ tsp coriander
- Salt and pepper to taste

Instructions:

1. Sauté onion and garlic in a pot.
2. Add lentils, broth, and spices.
3. Simmer for 25–30 minutes until lentils are tender.

Hero's Feast Stuffed Mushrooms

Ingredients:

- 12 large mushrooms, stems removed
- ½ cup cream cheese
- ¼ cup Parmesan cheese
- 2 cloves garlic, minced
- 1 tbsp chopped parsley
- ½ tsp black pepper

Instructions:

1. Preheat oven to 375°F (190°C).
2. Mix cream cheese, Parmesan, garlic, parsley, and pepper.
3. Stuff mushrooms with mixture.
4. Bake for 15–20 minutes.

Eternal Flame Baked Brie

Ingredients:

- 1 wheel of Brie cheese
- ¼ cup honey
- ¼ cup chopped nuts (almonds, pecans, or walnuts)
- ½ tsp cinnamon
- Puff pastry (optional)

Instructions:

1. Preheat oven to 375°F (190°C).
2. Place Brie on a baking sheet (or wrap in puff pastry).
3. Drizzle with honey and sprinkle with nuts and cinnamon.
4. Bake for 15 minutes.

Selene's Moonlit Lavender Lemonade

Ingredients:

- 4 cups water
- ½ cup lemon juice
- ¼ cup honey
- 1 tsp dried culinary lavender

Instructions:

1. Heat 1 cup of water and steep lavender for 5 minutes.
2. Strain, then mix with lemon juice, honey, and remaining water.
3. Serve chilled over ice.

Nectarous Apricot Almond Tart

Ingredients:

- 1 sheet puff pastry
- ½ cup apricot jam
- 4 fresh apricots, sliced
- ¼ cup sliced almonds
- 1 tbsp honey

Instructions:

1. Preheat oven to 375°F (190°C).
2. Spread apricot jam over puff pastry. Arrange apricot slices on top.
3. Sprinkle with almonds and drizzle with honey.
4. Bake for 20–25 minutes.

Circe's Enchanted Herb Butter

Ingredients:

- ½ cup unsalted butter, softened
- 1 tbsp fresh basil, chopped
- 1 tbsp fresh parsley, chopped
- 1 tsp fresh thyme
- ½ tsp garlic powder
- Salt to taste

Instructions:

1. Mix all ingredients together.
2. Chill and serve with bread or grilled meats.

Hercules' Power Lentil Stew

Ingredients:

- 1 cup green or brown lentils
- 4 cups vegetable broth
- 1 small onion, diced
- 2 carrots, chopped
- 2 celery stalks, chopped
- 3 cloves garlic, minced
- 1 can diced tomatoes (14 oz)
- 1 tsp cumin
- 1 tsp smoked paprika
- ½ tsp black pepper
- ½ tsp salt
- 1 tbsp olive oil
- 1 handful fresh spinach (optional)

Instructions:

1. Heat olive oil in a large pot over medium heat. Sauté onion, carrots, and celery for 5 minutes.
2. Add garlic, cumin, paprika, salt, and pepper. Stir for 1 minute.
3. Add lentils, broth, and tomatoes. Simmer for 30 minutes until lentils are tender.
4. Stir in spinach before serving.

Orion's Constellation Berry Tart

Ingredients:

- 1 pre-made tart shell
- 1 cup mixed berries (blueberries, raspberries, blackberries)
- ½ cup cream cheese, softened
- ¼ cup powdered sugar
- 1 tsp vanilla extract
- ¼ cup apricot jam (for glaze)

Instructions:

1. Mix cream cheese, powdered sugar, and vanilla until smooth. Spread over tart shell.
2. Arrange berries in a starry pattern.
3. Warm apricot jam and brush over berries for a glossy finish.
4. Chill before serving.

Eros' Passionfruit Mousse

Ingredients:

- 1 cup passionfruit pulp
- ½ cup heavy cream
- ½ cup condensed milk
- 1 tsp vanilla extract
- 1 tsp gelatin powder
- 2 tbsp warm water

Instructions:

1. Dissolve gelatin in warm water and let it sit for 5 minutes.
2. Blend passionfruit pulp, condensed milk, and vanilla.
3. Whip heavy cream until soft peaks form, then fold into passionfruit mixture.
4. Stir in gelatin and mix well. Chill for 2 hours before serving.

Celestial Honeycomb Parfait

Ingredients:

- 1 cup Greek yogurt
- ½ cup granola
- ¼ cup honeycomb pieces
- ¼ cup fresh berries

Instructions:

1. Layer yogurt, granola, and honeycomb in a glass.
2. Top with fresh berries and drizzle with extra honey if desired.

Underworld Spiced Dark Chocolate

Ingredients:

- 1 cup dark chocolate (70% cocoa or higher)
- ½ tsp cayenne pepper
- ½ tsp cinnamon
- ¼ tsp sea salt

Instructions:

1. Melt chocolate over a double boiler or microwave in short bursts.
2. Stir in cayenne, cinnamon, and sea salt.
3. Pour into a mold or spread on parchment paper. Let set before breaking into pieces.

Pegasus' Fluffy Cloud Pancakes

Ingredients:

- 1 cup flour
- 1 tbsp sugar
- 1 tsp baking powder
- ½ tsp baking soda
- 1 cup buttermilk
- 1 egg
- 1 tbsp melted butter
- 1 tsp vanilla extract

Instructions:

1. Mix flour, sugar, baking powder, and baking soda.
2. Whisk buttermilk, egg, melted butter, and vanilla in a separate bowl.
3. Combine wet and dry ingredients, stirring gently.
4. Cook pancakes on a greased skillet until golden.

Pandora's Surprise Truffle Box

Ingredients:

- 1 cup dark chocolate, melted
- ½ cup heavy cream
- ¼ cup assorted fillings (chopped nuts, dried fruit, caramel, sea salt)
- Cocoa powder for rolling

Instructions:

1. Heat heavy cream and pour over melted chocolate. Stir until smooth.
2. Let cool slightly, then fold in assorted fillings.
3. Chill for 1 hour, then roll into small balls. Coat in cocoa powder.

Mount Olympus Date and Nut Bars

Ingredients:

- 1 cup dates, pitted
- ½ cup almonds
- ½ cup walnuts
- 1 tbsp honey
- ½ tsp cinnamon

Instructions:

1. Blend dates, nuts, honey, and cinnamon in a food processor.
2. Press mixture into a lined baking dish.
3. Chill for 1 hour before slicing into bars.

Gilded Thyme-Infused Roast Duck

Ingredients:

- 1 whole duck (about 4-5 lbs)
- 2 tbsp olive oil
- 2 tbsp fresh thyme, chopped
- 1 tbsp honey
- 1 tbsp balsamic vinegar
- 3 cloves garlic, minced
- 1 tsp salt
- ½ tsp black pepper
- 1 orange, sliced

Instructions:

1. Preheat oven to 375°F (190°C).
2. Pat the duck dry and score the skin in a crisscross pattern.
3. Rub olive oil, thyme, honey, balsamic vinegar, garlic, salt, and pepper all over the duck.
4. Stuff the cavity with orange slices.
5. Place in a roasting pan and cook for 1.5-2 hours, basting occasionally.
6. Let rest before slicing.

Aeolus' Whirlwind Citrus Salad

Ingredients:

- 1 grapefruit, segmented
- 1 orange, segmented
- 1 blood orange, segmented
- ¼ red onion, thinly sliced
- ¼ cup pomegranate seeds
- ¼ cup feta cheese, crumbled
- 2 tbsp fresh mint leaves
- 2 tbsp olive oil
- 1 tbsp honey
- ½ tsp sea salt
- ¼ tsp black pepper

Instructions:

1. Arrange citrus segments on a plate.
2. Scatter red onion, pomegranate seeds, feta, and mint over the top.
3. Drizzle with olive oil and honey, then sprinkle with salt and pepper.

Golden Chariot Roasted Squash

Ingredients:

- 1 butternut squash, peeled and cubed
- 2 tbsp olive oil
- 1 tbsp maple syrup
- 1 tsp cinnamon
- ½ tsp nutmeg
- ½ tsp salt
- ¼ cup toasted pecans

Instructions:

1. Preheat oven to 400°F (200°C).
2. Toss squash cubes with olive oil, maple syrup, cinnamon, nutmeg, and salt.
3. Spread on a baking sheet and roast for 30-35 minutes.
4. Sprinkle with toasted pecans before serving.

Ambrosia Caramelized Figs with Yogurt

Ingredients:

- 6 fresh figs, halved
- 2 tbsp honey
- 1 tbsp butter
- ½ tsp cinnamon
- 1 cup Greek yogurt
- ¼ cup chopped pistachios

Instructions:

1. Melt butter in a skillet over medium heat.
2. Add figs, drizzle with honey, and sprinkle with cinnamon. Cook for 3-5 minutes until caramelized.
3. Serve over Greek yogurt and top with pistachios.

Hestia's Hearth Baked Apple Dumplings

Ingredients:

- 2 large apples, cored and halved
- 1 sheet puff pastry, thawed
- 2 tbsp brown sugar
- 1 tsp cinnamon
- 1 tbsp butter, melted
- 1 egg, beaten

Instructions:

1. Preheat oven to 375°F (190°C).
2. Mix brown sugar and cinnamon. Coat apple halves in melted butter, then roll in the sugar mixture.
3. Wrap each apple half in puff pastry, sealing the edges.
4. Brush with egg wash and bake for 25-30 minutes until golden brown.

Aurora's Sunrise Mango Sorbet

Ingredients:

- 2 cups frozen mango chunks
- ½ cup orange juice
- 2 tbsp honey
- 1 tsp lime juice

Instructions:

1. Blend all ingredients until smooth.
2. Freeze for 1-2 hours before serving.

Nectar-Soaked Almond Pastries

Ingredients:

- 1 sheet phyllo dough, thawed
- ½ cup ground almonds
- ¼ cup honey
- 2 tbsp butter, melted
- ½ tsp cinnamon

Instructions:

1. Preheat oven to 350°F (175°C).
2. Brush phyllo dough with melted butter and sprinkle with almonds and cinnamon.
3. Roll tightly, cut into small pieces, and bake for 15-20 minutes.
4. Drizzle with warm honey before serving.

www.ingramcontent.com/pod-product-compliance
Lightning Source LLC
LaVergne TN
LVHW061955070526
838199LV00060B/4134